Freedom
Mindset

Brian Robben

ISBN-10: 1530361443

ISBN-13: 978-1530361441

Contents

Important: Get Your Checklist......................iv

Introduction v

1. Money Coming In....................................... 1

2. The Most Important Factor To Becoming Rich... 13

3. Destroying Debt....................................... 18

4. Saving For Freedom.................................. 28

5. Spending With A Plan............................... 39

6. Investing Truths And Myths..................... 47

7. Your Winning Investment Strategy........... 54

8. Feed The Investing Machine..................... 65

9. Remember The Goal: Financial Freedom.......... 71

10. Follow Through For Success 77

More From Brian Robben............................. 80

Important: Get Your Checklist

As a special thanks to my readers, I created The Freedom Mindset Checklist. This checklist will improve your reading experience and help you follow through with the book's main action steps.

To get the most value out of this book and the time you spend reading it, go to TakeYourSuccess.com/checklist. I timed myself and it took 15 seconds to get there, so you can do the same. Get the checklist now before you forget!

Introduction

How often do you wish you had more money? Maybe you wish you had a bigger bank account so you had the freedom to travel. Maybe you wish you could afford a new car or a nicer place. Maybe you go to work for a paycheck, but wish you had your dream job. Maybe you want to pay off your student loans or retire early. Maybe you wish you didn't cringe every time you checked your dwindling bank account the morning after a night out. When you stop and think about it, the list of things we need money for gets overwhelming. And, sometimes, it can all pile up. You can feel like financial peace is impossible. You can feel trapped.

You're not the only one. A lot of young adults worry about money. It's normal to worry about trying to make it in a world that revolves around how much money you have, or don't have, and what you can spend it on.

But wouldn't it be nice to not worry about money? To not be trapped? Wouldn't it be freeing to become so rich that you don't even think about making money—but instead, you think about pursuing happiness?

That's where this book comes in. It's full of advice to fight and resolve those money worries. With the easy-to-follow strategies, you can turn all those financial wishes into a reality.

That's the perfect situation you're looking for, right? You get to grow your money and live the lifestyle you've dreamed of, without spending all of your time focusing on your bank account. Soon, I'll show you how to do that.

But first, let me tell you why I'm the best person to walk you through those money worries. I'm not a financial planner, accountant, or investment banker. Heck, I didn't major in business in college. I'm a 23-year-old recent college grad who majored in English.

Sure, I'm 23 and don't have these financial certifications—but that actually plays to my advantage. I can give you tried and true money advice, and here's why:

First, I'm in the thick of things with you. I know what it's like to have no money and want more. I can relate to getting a real job, and trying to manage money when there are so many financial choices to be made. And, I have strong desires to become financially independent, so I can live a rich and full life and find freedom with my choices.

Second, I've read hundreds of articles and books about money, and then implemented the strategies to build my net worth. It feels great to have strong financial intelligence and be in control over my money, instead of being stuck without answers and at the mercy of others.

Third and most importantly, I'm writing from a place of experience. I didn't have all the teaching on this, so I had to seek it out for myself. And, I wrote with your perspective in mind. As I picked and chose what you really needed to know, I avoided the less significant noise that will only confuse and discourage you. What's in this book are the quick and reliable truths of growing money when you're young.

Because I spent years reading complex personal finance ideas, I can now break these concepts down into simple ideas to help you take action and reach your financial goals. If you go deep into almost any money topic, it's easy to get quickly confused and then paralyzed about what to do next.

That's why this book is designed to fight financial confusion (which leads to negative inaction), by giving you clear financial tips (which leads to positive action).

I believe young adults need to understand simple money principles, and then take simple actions. When it comes down to it, it will take a couple of hours to get on the right path to a rich, free, and satisfying life.

College students, grad students, and young professionals across the country have already implemented the strategies in this book for great financial success. How do I know? They're my friends and people I've met through my blog about these techniques.

For example, Benjamin, a grad student at the University of Michigan, says, "Brian's book is extremely helpful because it's exactly to the point, but doesn't sacrifice any value in its simplicity. Follow these money strategies and you can't miss freedom."

And Megan, a young professional in Chicago, says, "Because of the actions I took from Freedom Mindset, I rest easy knowing my money is working for me on autopilot until I'm a millionaire one day. Brian crushed this one."

With huge results from others and myself, I promise that if you implement the step-by-step approach in this book, you'll become rich enough to retire when you want to. And I promise that you will be able to stop spending the majority of your time trying to make an income. So you can spend your time doing what you want, blessing others with your money, and not worrying about money.

But, all of these rewards are in jeopardy if you put off reading this for another time. We all know another time could turn into a year, a decade, or a lifetime of missing out on financial freedom.

Don't be the person who wastes an amazing opportunity and lives with regret. Be the person who has a plan for their money. Be the person who finds answers to take charge of their money immediately. Be the person who breaks free to live in freedom.

To avoid any possible confusion, this is not the book for those who are looking for investing advice on shorting the Brazilian real estate market, or want tips to make a million dollars next week from penny stocks.

However, this is the book for you if you want easy steps to become rich. Spend a couple of hours reading this book and a couple of hours implementing the action steps, and you're on your way to becoming a millionaire. Now is the time to get started!

Checklist Reminder

Before we actually get started, I want to stop and give you another chance to download the checklist for this book. I made the process quick and easy for you, just visit here:

TakeYourSuccess.com/checklist

Chapter 1

Money Coming In

I remember seeing my first full-time paycheck just after college. I must have looked like I had bug eyes when I woke up and checked my bank account that first payday.

I had summer jobs and internships before, but this full-time paycheck totaled more than I made all summer at my previous internship and then some. I've never been paid that much for only weeks of work.

For the first time in my life, I had an excess of money and didn't exactly know what to do with it. All I knew is that I didn't want to blow it. I had a dream for my paycheck, and for all my future income—freedom.

I never want to feel trapped by how much money I'm making or not making. I don't want to hang on every paycheck as a way to make it through. I want to build wealth. I want to find a career I love. I want financial freedom. To me, that means seeing my income as a tool—something to grow and nourish. It means following a plan and working toward a place where I don't worry (or think twice) about money, because I've set myself up that way. I can afford the life I want and not worry about the future. I can be free.

Because of this dream for freedom, I read and studied as much material on creating wealth and millionaires as I could get my hands on. And I talked to people who created a wealth like that for themselves.

So, you might be wondering what I did with this money and every paycheck after all of my research. You'll find out soon enough.

One of my first missions as a young professional was to get rich. It might sound corny, but I believe having wealth leads to a healthy lifestyle. How does that happen? It's not rocket science to understand that you need some type of income to become rich. Earning money is the driving force that affects how you save, invest, and spend your money.

Making money is also good for the soul. When you're paid for the value of your work, you get a personal sense of pride, accomplishment, and well-being. As cliche as it sounds, you feel like a worthwhile and contributing member of society. And when you get paid, it validates all of the years you spent getting an education.

On the flip side, life can suck when there isn't enough money coming in. You may start to feel sick and become depressed. It can also be a nightmare when you don't have the resources to pay for life's essentials: housing, car payment, insurance, and food. And feeling like a failure to your friends, your family, and yourself creates all sorts of negative vibes you don't want.

For your wealth and your well-being, the sections below are designed to increase your income. The more money you bring in will also support the steps in the following chapters, so please read closely.

Earning Power

Let's say you have a full-time job. If you're like 99% of people, the income from your job will be your most valuable financial asset. To some extent, that steady stream of income gives you considerable control and comfort in your life.

When you're guaranteed a paycheck every two weeks, it seems reasonable to make future plans with your money and upgrade your lifestyle. However, not to be Mr. Negative, but I have to crash your party a little bit. Your salary most likely isn't as stable as you imagine.

There are countless situations outside of your control where you're left without a job. Here's a few examples: Say another economic recession happens, your organization decides to downsize, or you simply underperform. As a young adult and new employee, you're most likely one of the first to get laid off or fired. And these scenarios don't mention the future possibilities of getting replaced by a smarter Chinese worker or even a robot—hey, don't underestimate technology.

In each of these cases, the salary you heavily rely on simply disappears. And when you get fired and lose the paycheck you desperately need, it hits you like a train—bam!

The point I'm making is to never get too comfortable with your salary, because job security is a thing of the past. People, businesses, and innovations move too fast nowadays to have the attitude that your job is forever stable.

Now that I crashed your party, I'm going to revive it and bring back the guests, alcohol, and music. Actually I'm going to give you three ideas to improve your earning power so you're always prepared for whatever life throws at you in terms of your income.

The first way to protect your earning power, or increase it, is to constantly keep learning. Educate yourself about topics related to your current job, and spend time learning about other subjects. As the future changes, you'll be ready for whatever comes because you stayed mentally sharp and thus kept your value.

It's the people who stop learning that get passed by and land on the chopping block at work. And if they get fired, other organizations don't want them either because their lack of knowledge makes them less valuable than someone else, or completely unvaluable.

Second, you need to continually improve your skills and marketability. Put what you're learning into action to gain experience. Keep testing what gets you the most success at work and what you can do less of to improve your overall value.

As your knowledge and skills increase, you become a versatile asset that will withstand any bad economy, layoff period, or firing. If you're talented and get fired, then it won't take time to get a new job. Ultimately, people who can drive enough value to their organization, coworkers, or customers are seemingly priceless. And they sometimes recognize their value so they go off to successfully work for themselves, adding to the idea that opportunities are abundant when you create value.

Speaking of working for themselves, there is a third option—create your own income stream. Start a side project to sell services you're good at, create a website like TakeYourSuccess.com, or create a product people are willing to buy.

Are you a decent writer, photographer, or artist? Do you have a large Instagram following and you're interested in consulting others on social media marketing? Have a blog and want to be a consultant on content marketing? Find anything you're already good at or interested in, put in some hard work to learn and then you will get paid for your skillset.

These all take time and practice to develop, but once you make money apart from your day job, you're protected from losing all your income if you lose your job. Or you create enough income on your side hustle that you can quit your day job to pursue it full time. I wish I could go into more detail, but this isn't an entrepreneurial business book. I may write one in the future, but there are other great articles and books out there on that subject.

Find And Get Paid Your Market Value

How nice and comfortable that regular salary paycheck is, right? Well, you may be wrong. Because when you have a salary, it's easy to rest on your laurels and go through life by the motions.

Resting easy isn't such a bad thing, except when it makes you soft and lazy toward earning what you're actually worth. And organizations aren't going to help you in that area.

Most companies aren't "in the business" of making sure every employee is paid their true market value. They're happy to pay you way less than what you're worth. They certainly don't want to pay you more than they have to.

This affects you because if you don't know your market value, you can work for years as you're making significantly less money than you deserve.

To find your market value, simply visit Glassdoor.com and create an account (or you can sign-in through Facebook). Then click the salary tab, type in your position, and the city where you work.

For example, I'm going to act as a recruiter who works in Chicago, IL and makes $40,000 a year.

Once the new screen loads, you'll first see the national salary average and local salary average for your position. In this example, the national salary average for a recruiter is $50,750, and the Chicago area average is $47,103.

Below this section on the page, you'll also see a large list of companies with the same position and the salary they pay to the right. Only compare the same exact position—and comparable companies if you can find them—to get a good idea of your market value. For my example, there's a difference between a recruiter and a technical recruiter, so comparing salaries of these two positions isn't as helpful.

Scroll through and click to see more companies and their salaries until you get a good idea if you're underpaid or adequately paid. I would shoot for around 10 different salaries to get a good idea.

After you determine your market value (you don't need an exact sum to the dollar, a range works), be honest with yourself to determine if you're well-paid or underpaid.

No matter if you're underpaid or well-paid and want to push yourself to make more money, the most practical way to increase your income is to negotiate your salary.

Eight Steps To Salary Negotiation Excellence

Whether you're negotiating your salary at a new job, or as a current employee, this one step is absolutely critical to making more money. Employees who don't negotiate their salary often leave $1,000 to $10,000 dollars on the table in their first year, when all they had to do is speak up a little. That's insane!

It also amazes me how many of my peers took the first salary offered to them. Maybe they were so excited to get an offer that they didn't care about their salary. But, I know they would act differently if they understood that their starting salary often affects how much they are paid throughout their career, which could lead to a difference of a million dollars.

Maybe they feared the organization would revoke their job offer if they tried to negotiate their salary and their request got taken the wrong way. Yet, organizations almost never take away a job offer since they spent thousands of dollars recruiting you and obviously want you enough to offer you the job in the first place.

Or maybe my friends were too uncomfortable to discuss a higher salary. But, think of it this way. Would you have a potentially uncomfortable conversation, that usually lasts no longer than 15 minutes, for $1,000? I know you would do it. And for $10,000 I could get you to talk about anything, even gross stuff, and of course you would do it.

The ironic factor is that many companies will actually be impressed by your confidence, assertiveness, and effort to negotiate your salary for more money, especially when you do it right. So, there's no question about negotiating your salary, because when you do it and do it well, easy money is waiting for you.

These are the key insights to negotiating your salary (and exactly what I used to get $10,000 more than my initial salary offer at my first job):

Step 1 - Know the salary you want, and what range you'll accept.
Assuming you already went on Glassdoor.com to find your market value, the minimum salary you would accept, and the salary you would be ecstatic about, now is time to narrow down the salary

you want. A good starting place is to talk to your friends with similar experience as you and similar jobs about how much money they're making. But honestly, you're going to find the most valuable information on what salary range to expect by speaking with someone you know at the company, if you have that option.

Knowing the minimum offer you would accept and your desired salary will help your decision-making during the next steps of the negotiation process.

Step 2 - Make them say the number first.

During the interview process, your impatience may tempt you to bring up salary before the recruiter. But, this is a big no-no! The old adage goes, "The first person who brings up money, loses," and this is still true. If you make them bring up the salary first, then you're in the driver's seat and have more negotiating power.

Be patient even if it turns into a chess game where you continually deflect and give back general answers. Wait until they say it first. Some helpful phrases when you're pressured to say a salary figure include:

- "I want a fair offer that benefits both of us."

- "I have a range in my head, but I want to see what you say first to make sure we're on the same page."

- "How about you tell me what you're thinking, and then I'll respond based on what I think is competitive."

Plus, when you make them say the number first, you never face the problem of prematurely bringing up salary and sending the wrong message that you only want the job for the money.

Step 3 - Use another job offer as leverage.

Another job offer is your most persuasive tactic in the game of salary negotiation, without a doubt. The company will immediately value you higher and want you more, which leads to an increased salary offer.

Start interviewing with multiple organizations at the same time to get another offer to tell the other companies about it. And if you have more than one job offer, that's even more negotiation power. For example, multiple job offers made the biggest difference when I negotiated my starting salary.

Step 4 - Be friendly during the process through body language.

The essence of negotiation is that you and the organization both get what they want: You want the job, and they want an employee who creates value for their organization. That's why when you keep a friendly demeanor throughout the process, you invite an open discussion to reach the shared goal of a fair agreement.

A great way to enforce your pleasant demeanor and show that you're cooperating is through your body language. Use open palms when speaking (shows you're trustworthy), smile (the universal language for kindness), and nod your head up and down while maintaining eye contact even if you disagree with what's being said (will decrease tension in the room).

Trying to bulldoze the other side in negotiations will do more harm than good. Because—keep in mind—you have to work with these people after the negotiation. And they will most likely have a say in your promotions and salary going forward. Don't be a jerk.

Step 5 - Ask, "Can you do better?"

If you're not satisfied with the current offer, you need to balance the fine line of asking for more money while still being a team player. The question, "Can you do better?" works well because it's non-aggressively communicating your desire, while empowering the manager to help you out. When you're asking for more money, the worst they can say is "no." And when you don't ask, the answer is already "no."

Step 6 - Negotiate for more than your salary.

Once the salary conversation concludes, next up are the non-cash job benefits to sweeten your offer. Depending on the job, some non-cash perks that are potentially negotiable include:

- Stock options
- Company car
- Mileage reimbursement
- Expense credit card
- Additional paid vacations
- Healthcare or dental plan
- Tuition reimbursement
- Moving costs
- Cell phone bills

Be strategic in negotiating for what non-cash benefit you really want, because you can't slam your fists on the table and demand them all. You will sound like a whiny kid at the store who says, "I want this, this, this, and that." Nobody wants to hire that person.

Go for one extra benefit (potentially two if you're confident they really want you), and give up the other perks to remain fair with the employer. As I previously said, this isn't a war room negotiation, because you'll have to work with these people when this is over.

Step 7 - Practice negotiation with your friends, your family, and yourself.

Before you ever get in the room to negotiate with the company, first practice negotiation as much as you can. Convince a friend to come over or Skype a family member by saying, "Here's the deal, I'll buy you Chipotle if you let me practice salary negotiation with you." If you're too uncomfortable to practice negotiation, then it's probably too awkward to add thousands of dollars to your salary, too. That was sarcastic, because come on! This is easy money in your pocket.

For extra practice, talk to yourself in the mirror as you monitor your body language and speak the negotiation tactics laid out above. Each time you practice will help you be less nervous and more effective during the real negotiation.

Step 8 - If you're not getting anywhere, then keep your cool and bring up a future raise.

Sometimes the company has a hard number that they can't move on, or the hiring manager's hands are tied by his or her boss. You haven't exhausted all of your negotiation options yet. The last thing you can do is say, "If I take this offer and perform extremely well, could we set a time in the next 6 to 12 months to discuss a raise?" Assuming they say yes and you set a specific time frame, be safe by making sure you get this renegotiation agreement in writing.

When Your Salary Negotiation Doesn't Work And You're Stuck

When you're worried their offer is too low, you have two options: you can either take the job at a lower salary, or decline this job for a different opportunity. If you do take the position, work your butt off in the beginning by going above and beyond expectations. The better your performance, the easier the salary negotiation will go when you have that discussion later on.

The second option is to realize that this isn't the only company in the world and to start looking at other organizations. And when it comes time to talk salary at a new job, use the same negotiation strategies above to earn what you're worth.

Action Steps

Summing up this chapter, these are the three action steps you can take to keep and improve your income:

- [ ] Improve your value by gaining industry knowledge and skills, taking on a new project, going through a course, reading career-related material and books, or doing freelance work on a side business.

- [ ] Check your market value every 12 months, and look for a raise or a new job if you're underpaid.

- [ ] Negotiate your salary when starting a new position or performing extremely well in your current position.

Chapter 2

The Most Important Factor To Becoming Rich

Before I dive in to this chapter, I have a question for you: What do you think is the single most important factor to becoming rich?

I'll give you ten seconds to think of an answer.

Time is up.

I'll bet that you said the best way to become rich is to make a lot of money. (If I'm right, you owe me a drink. If I'm wrong, then I owe you one.)

How did I know you were going to answer something around the idea of "making a lot of money"? It's because American culture obsesses over the idea of making a boatload of money in a short amount of time.

For example, the reason the Floyd Mayweather and Manny Pacquiao fight received an insane amount of media attention is not because of the fight itself but the absurd amount of money involved.

For 36 minutes of boxing, reports say Floyd Mayweather made around $200 to $220 million. If you're not doing the math, Mayweather made $5.5 million per minute, when using the conservative $200 million figure.

And then, there are the millions of people who buy scratch-off tickets, hoping to win big in a matter of seconds. There's always the lingering hope that you'll instantly win the lottery and not have to worry about the future. Winning big in a small amount of time sounds great—but the odds are not in your favor. Sorry about that.

I used to think this way, too. I thought I could get rich quick by betting on National Football League games when I was a junior in college.

I had a friend that was a bookie, and each week I placed multiple $100 bets on NFL games. I did well and cashed out winning $200, $450, and more on certain weeks. After these quick wins, I dreamed of making millions of dollars as I placed bets poolside in my mansion. I thought that could be a reality.

Then one week, the dream crashed. I lost a streak of close games, and went in the hole around $1,200. If the loss didn't sting enough, it became worse when I was short the money and needed to pay up in two days.

Fortunately I knew this guy, so I didn't fear for my life when I told him it was going to take me months to pay him back. But, if that was a ruthless bookie that I didn't know and I didn't pay on the collection date, it could have cost me my life. No joke.

I learned my lesson about gambling and trying to get rich quick the hard way. However, I know many of my friends and family still believe the best way to wealth is making a lot of money in a short amount of time.

It's a myth that to become rich you have to earn a six- or seven-figure income. Making a lot of money can certainly help your financial situation, but it's not the most important aspect.

The most important factor to becoming rich is wise money management.

You might say, "Brian, what does that even mean, dude? That's such a vague and boring answer." I agree that making a million dollars a year to become rich is way sexier than smart money management.

However, I'm positive you will agree that having financial intelligence is the best route to becoming rich. Let me explain, dude.

Wise Money Management

It seems athletes always get picked on, doesn't it? So, I figure it won't hurt if I add onto the pile to support my case.

To attack the point that the best way to become rich is to make a lot of money, I present to the jury Exhibit A: Mike Tyson, Exhibit B: Evander Holyfield, and Exhibit C: Allen Iverson.

Former heavyweight boxing champion of the world Mike Tyson went bankrupt after blowing through around $300 million on mansions, jewelry, partying, and even pet tigers. The three tigers cost a total of $210,000, plus $200,000 in food, and $125,000 a year for the animal handler.

Another boxing world champion and legend, Evander Holyfield, lost his estimated $230 million piggy bank through unwise financial decisions. Holyfield purchased a 109-room house, had a loan for $550,000 in landscaping, and a ridiculously high alimony to three ex-wives plus child support for 11 kids.

The 11-time NBA All-Star Allen Iverson burned through $150 million in career earnings like the money was on fire. Iverson destroyed his fortune on multiple mortgages, jewelry, designer clothes, entertainment (balling out at the club), and supporting his entourage of around 50 people.

And those are only a few examples of countless others I could have grabbed where people made millions of dollars and are bankrupt now.

Where did these athletes and other high-income earners go down the wrong path?

The reason why the three athletes above and so many other people commonly go broke is they haven't developed smart money management. And a lack of financial intelligence isn't only an athlete problem, it's everywhere.

You don't hear about pharmaceutical rep Joe Schmo who makes $100,000 a year but is treading water in debt after overspending on cars, vacations, and houses because Joe isn't famous and didn't lose $20 million. Yet, it's the same problem stemming from a lack of wisdom about money.

No matter how much money is made—one-hundred thousand, one million, one-hundred million—it's going to soon disappear if you're not financially intelligent. This is why the act of making big money isn't the best way to become rich. In this fashion, you can be rich in an instant and easily be fooled to think you'll be rich forever just because. And then you become broke in seemingly the next day.

But, when you're a wise money manager, you can make $50,000 a year the rest of your life and become a millionaire. The approach of implementing financial intelligence will give you riches and freedom without fooling you and causing you to lose everything in the future.

Before you get the feeling that you have to be a financial genius to implement wise money management, take a deep breath. Give that thought a hard kick on the way out of your mind.

In the next chapter, you'll start to discover the path to becoming rich. It's not what you think, because it's simple and automatic when you handle your money the right way.

There aren't any action steps in this chapter, just remember solid financial intelligence is the most important factor to becoming rich.

Chapter 3

Destroying Debt

A big part of becoming rich and reaching financial freedom is getting rid of what's holding you back: your debt.

And for young adults, the two most common roads to heavy debt are student loans and credit cards.

There is no doubt about this: Debt is your number one enemy. Debt is the big wall standing between you and your shot at ever being financially free. Maybe you have debt for a good reason, like college or buying a car you need to get around. Maybe you think debt isn't so bad. Everybody has it, right?

Let me get real. Debt is horrible. You should avoid it all costs, like a plague. Debt sets you up for pain and a limited life. Debt can trap you more than anything else money-related.

If you remember anything in this chapter, remember debt will get in your way of becoming rich and can single-handedly ruin your financial freedom.

Let the following example teach you why rich people don't do debt and why that's the first place to send your income to get out of it.

Debt Is The Worst Stage Five Clinger

The funny thing about debt is it can be like the stage five clinger that won't go away. You know what I'm talking about, right? You went to a party and there's some guy or girl you met. You're having a good time, appreciate the attention they're giving you, and although you know you might regret it, you decide to hook up with them at the end of the night.

It was only one impulse decision, so you think what's the harm. Little do you know, this person is obsessed with you now and can't go a day without asking you to hang out as they plan the rest of their life with you. They already love you, while you're thinking that escalated way too fast with this stage five clinger.

But, debt is the worst clinger you will ever meet because it chains you and your money. Then it makes your life unnecessarily difficult for decades. For example, say you splurge $2,000 on a vacation you can't afford, but hope to pay off later. The moment you charge your credit card, debt sets its trap. If you're unable to pay your monthly credit card bill, then you'll be charged a 20% annual interest rate on this amount. And then you might get stuck in a negative cycle of more bad decisions. So what starts out as a $2,000 mistake can easily snowball over five years to $40,000 in credit card debt. The credit card company is laughing to the bank, while you're trying to put the pieces of your life together after this financial disaster.

Or, even if you're in debt because of a responsible decision to go to college, your student loans can mess with your life for decades. This debt can disrupt your peace after every email reminder and monthly payment. Not only that: debt makes you worry about money, work longer in life, and live less happy.

So, like you would address the stage five clinger to back off, it's time to be straightforward with debt by saying, "I want nothing to do with you, get out of my life." That's the first step.

Step two, which is easier said than done, is to take action to get debt out of your life and free yourself from its chains.

Mission: Destroy Your Debt

Because debt can be vicious if you let it get out of control, I laid out a plan below to aggressively attack each debt.

But before we get started, we need to get in the right mental place. So, close your eyes and think of yourself as a NAVY Seal in a secret ops mission. You have your night vision goggles on with your assault rifle loaded and nothing is getting in your way to complete the mission because you're 100% focused.

Now, keep the focus and treat debt the same way by using the three objectives below to get started and become debt-free.

Objective 1: Eliminate Student Loans

Paying back student loans sucks, and it literally sucks away money that could have gone to invest and grow your wealth. So here are the steps to eliminate your student debt and remove this negative weight from your life.

1. Pay every two weeks instead of monthly.

This is a trick that is used to pay off a house sooner, but it works just as well for your student loans. You likely won't notice the difference in your checking account when you pay biweekly, but you will more importantly cut years off your student debt and save yourself thousands of dollars in interest.

This simple example shows how it works. Say your student loan payment is $190 a month. Ordinarily, you would pay $190 each month and pay off $2,280 in one year.

However, if you instead break this monthly payment in half to pay $95 every two weeks, you actually pay off $2,470 in one year. So paying biweekly helps you put an extra monthly payment of $190 toward your debt. This is true since there are 52 weeks in a year, you'd make 26 half payments, and therefore 13 full payments. And this extra payment each year will snowball into cutting years off of your payment plan and saving you thousands of dollars in interest.

2. Make larger payments.

You can absolutely improve your debt situation by making larger payments than what's required. I recommend you add anywhere from $50 to $200 to your biweekly payment. You might think $50 biweekly doesn't make much of a difference, but think of it this way: Small dents over time lead to a big dent and some confidence for your psyche, and this results in a future debt balance of zero.

I realize making larger payments might be hard given your other expenses. But, that's why it's so important to find avenues to increase your income or cut spending when you're in debt. Do a freelance project or a side hustle to get extra cash. Get pizza on Friday night instead of a downtown dinner to use the savings to pay off more debt. It won't be easy. But don't forget, if this was easy then you wouldn't be in this position from the start.

3. Set up automatic payments.

The biggest benefit of scheduling automatic payments from your checking account to the loan service is you will never have the money in your hands to spend it. An automatic payment provides a safe buffer to protect you from temptation. This also gives you certainty that you won't miss a payment and get penalized. Plus, setting this up will save you time every two weeks when you otherwise would have had to make time to manually pay.

Objective 2: Terminate Credit Card Debt

If you're in credit card debt, no matter how much or little, use the following five steps to climb out and clear a major obstacle on your path to becoming rich.

1. Tally the losses.

You might believe ignorance is bliss when it comes to not knowing how much credit card debt you have, but paying off your debt to zero is worth the short-term pain of facing the total number. It may require overcoming your fear, but being unaware of your balance leads to passively paying credit card bills each month with no strategic rhyme or reason, or hope. Talk about depressing.

Once you realize what you're up against, we can start cutting away at the debt and create some positive energy to eliminate the burden. To get the ball rolling and know how much debt you have, there are two options. Option 1 is to go online to each credit card company where you have debt, and note the total debt, APR (Annual Percentage Rate), and minimum monthly payment. Option 2 is to simply call the number on the back of your credit card and have them tell you these three things. The example exercise below shows what you should have when you've completed this step.

Example exercise:

Card	Total Debt	APR	Minimum Monthly Payment
Visa	$10,758	11.7%	$430.32
MasterCard	$7,881	14.9%	$315.24

Card	Total Debt	APR	Minimum Monthly Payment
Discover	$2,253	16.9%	$90.12

Doing this is important for the following steps, so it's in your best interest not to skip it.

2. Renegotiate your interest rates.

The APR is arguably the most frustrating part of credit card debt, because it uses compound interest (interest added on the initial figure and the accumulated interest) against you. However, believe it or not, you have more power than you think to decrease your interest rate and save yourself big money.

Take 10 minutes total out of your day, only one time, to call each credit card company where you have debt. Tell each company this same exact thing over the phone: you're going to start paying off your credit card debt sooner; but your interest rate is too high; and you want them to lower it.

If they pushback and say they can't do that, then say you have competitive interest rates 50% lower than your current rate from other companies, and again ask the person on the phone if they can match the 50% lower APR rate.

If the person on the line doesn't agree to cut your rate, you still have ammo to say the last thing they want to hear. Tell them if they really can't lower your rates, then you will close your account this week and move your balance to another company with a better APR.

Do the steps above, and you can most likely come out with a 50% lower interest rate or no interest rate at all. If you're successful in cutting your rates, remember to edit the APR in the list from step 1.

This plan is worth a shot—the payoff can potentially save you thousands of dollars.

3. Choose what credit card balance to eliminate first.

If you have multiple credit card balances, I recommend first focusing on paying off the card with the highest APR, and paying the minimum monthly payment for the other cards. Besides sending most of your paycheck to your debts, it also helps to send any extra money that comes your way. Extra money includes a bonus from work, birthday money, or any savings that you can use to lower the card with the highest APR rate. Once that balance is at zero, do the same with your next highest APR rate (while paying the monthly minimum on the remaining cards) and so on until you're completely out of credit card debt.

4. Stop using your credit cards.

To avoid taking one step forward and two steps backward, it's time to stop using your credit cards so you don't add to your debt total. Take your credit cards out of your wallet or purse, and put them in a safe place in your room until your debt is clear.

Psychologically, you will spend less using cash for purchases instead of credit cards. Spending less obviously results in having more money to pay off your balances. Also, you begin to train yourself to develop better spending habits when instant gratification isn't a swipe away. Exercising consumer discipline will get you to pay off your debt sooner and stay out of debt in the future.

I disagree with some personal finance experts who recommend cancelling the credit cards after paying them off, because that will negatively affect your credit score. I'll cover more about your credit score later in this chapter.

5. Start paying your balances off today.

Besides avoiding more damaging moves—like taking out another loan, missing other bills, or taking money out of your investment accounts—the best step for future freedom is to take immediate strides to pay off these balances. It will take time to pay off these debts, so I recommend getting started and doing these five steps right now. But if you need more time, don't let the next weekend go by without doing this.

For those who are extremely committed, start packing your lunch, cut out some unnecessary entertainment, and look for other ways to save money to pay off more debt. Let your mindset be if you can't feel the pain (meaning your life is just as comfortable as before), then you're not sacrificing enough. The sooner you're debt-free, the sooner you'll be on your way to becoming rich and financially free.

Objective 3: Stay Out Of Debt

If you're fortunate enough to be debt-free and want to stay out of debt, use the following steps to protect your financial freedom.

1. Consider the opportunity cost of your monthly payment and debt.

Buying something new that you have to go in debt for isn't only an immediate setback, but this move will also cost you future money-making opportunities. Because every monthly payment that goes to debt is money that could have been used as an investment to grow your wealth.

2. Before you make a big purchase, ask yourself, "Is this a want or a need?"

Your college education, the car you need for work, and your apartment or house are probably needs. But, new clothes, a huge television, and swanky headphones are wants that you can live without for now—and they're going to depreciate over time. Plus, when you spend money on these material items, they often come with huge interest rates if you can't pay them off right away.

3. Don't spend out of social pressure.

Many people spend above their means because of other people. When you're under the impression that you need to keep up with the purchases of your friends, coworkers, or neighbors, you increase the chances of being just like them—scraping by each month or in debt, which is miles away from freedom.

Instead of passively deciding not to hang with your friends without giving a reason, the better solution is to be honest. Tell them, "I'd love to, but I need to save my money right now." If they're that upset you can't go to happy hour with them every week, or you're not comfortable enough to speak up, then they might not be the best of friends.

4. Check your credit score at least once a year and improve it.

One number, your credit score, can make the difference in whether you get a car loan, an apartment or house loan, and sometimes a job (companies use your credit score to judge how responsible you are). Also, your credit score can save or cost you thousands of dollars a year based on what homeowner and insurance rates you receive. That's why your credit score can make a big difference in helping you stay out of debt. Check out your credit score for free with one of these options: www.CreditKarma.com, www.Lending-Tree.com, or www.Credit.com.

To protect your credit score or improve it: pay off your entire credit card bill each month, don't use more than 30% of your monthly credit limit, let your credit card length age over time (nothing you can do here besides wait), and don't cancel any credit cards (even if you're not using them).

Action Steps

These are the main action steps from this chapter for you to get rid of debt:

☐ Figure out how much money you owe and increase your monthly payment by at least $100 a month.

☐ Set up biweekly automatic payments from your bank account to pay off your student loans debt.

☐ Pay off your credit card debt, and then credit card bill every month, through scheduling automatic payments.

Chapter 4

Saving For Freedom

Ready for some good news?

Here it is: As long as you're getting paid full-time from somewhere, you're most likely making enough money to achieve a rich life of financial freedom.

You got it? No matter the size of your paycheck, your current full-time income is probably enough to pave the path to millionaire status.

It's time to believe this truth and begin your journey to wealth today. A lot of people my age think the money they're making now isn't enough to start planning with. They're just happy to have excess money to spend on entertainment and clothes. So, many decide to wait until they make more money or until they're 35 before they start taking the money they bring in seriously.

But here's the thing. If you don't take your money seriously now, you will be significantly behind when you start. It's easy to put it off. But starting that saving-mentality now means a life of wealth and freedom is closer—and you'll make less mistakes along the way. This speeds up the process.

Your Current Saving Problem

Your parents, the media, and society tell you to save money. Young adults get this idea ingrained in their brain as something they should do, but we all know how many things we don't do that we should. We should floss, we should call our parents more, we should keep our room clean. But do we? Most of the time this answer is no.

And the same applies to twentysomethings with money. You know you should save but you don't. Why don't you? It's probably because saving money for the sake of saving money isn't fun. Who wants to put money aside for no real reason? It's not an inspiring mindset. And your motivation to save will have no match when immediate gratification comes knocking and asks you to spend your money.

Are you going to save your money because you feel like you're supposed to? Or are you going to buy the new watch, clothes, or car? Most people choose the instant pleasure and unknowingly sacrifice an amazing future because of their daily choices to spend more and save less. Then these bad decisions force them to work until they're 65, 70, or 75, as they wonder how their neighbor retired at 40 and has the freedom to do what he wants.

But, what if you believed you were saving your money for something different? Something that will actually make you happier and is so valuable that it's arguably the most desired treasure of all.

What if you changed your mindset to save for freedom? The beautiful, glorious, and insanely attractive reality of freedom.

Financial Freedom

The mindset to save for the sake of saving will almost always lose in comparison to other more tempting purchases. However, when you save for freedom, it's a whole new mental game. And if you're anything like me, freedom is more valuable than eating out every weekend or buying stuff. These purchases will give you a short-term rush of happiness, but this feeling soon fades. There's no price tag for freedom and its lasting happiness, so it always wins in comparison to instant gratification.

What do I mean by saving for freedom? Here's what I mean. When you save as much money as you can in the present, you free yourself in the future to spend time doing what you love regardless if it makes you money or not. At some point, you won't be working with the sole (and soul-draining) purpose of putting money in the bank. You'll work, or not work, because it's what you want to do. You'll have money saved, and you won't worry about the monthly bills, affording vacations, or the next big expense slated for five years down the road. You'll live your life freely—not stuck in the chains of making money.

What does that look like? With a high enough savings percentage, your money will open the door for you to freely: travel the world, get bottle service whenever you want (if that's your thing), flick your boss off and bust down your office doors at any moment (not my goal, but probably fun for some people), pick the job you want over the higher-paying job, or decide to follow your dreams without working a typical job because you don't need the money.

Those are a few examples of the opportunities that present themselves when you're financially free. Because when you save enough, you can invest and compound your money to the point where it grows for you on autopilot. (Investing is the subject of a later chapter, so be patient for now.)

So are you going to save for freedom? If you are, it all boils down to this: the earlier you save and the more you save of your income, the closer you are to glorious freedom. If you want true satisfaction from a financially free lifestyle instead of the average life where you're tied down working somewhere you probably dislike for the next 40 years, eat up these next sections and put them into action.

The Golden Savings Rule: Pay Yourself First

Even if you're super committed to saving for freedom, there will be times where you don't have the discipline to save money or invest money. But, there's an easy way to make sure you don't get in your own way of becoming rich. It's called automatically paying yourself first.

What I call The Golden Savings Rule, paying yourself first means that when money comes in, you already have a system set up that automatically transfers a certain percentage of the money to another account to save or invest. That money is going to the future you—and future you is very grateful, already! After making the first decision on how much you're going to save each month, the money comes in and then instantly goes where you want it to without having to think about it. This automation makes saving effortless, requires no discipline or hard choices, and basically forces your hand to become rich. Talk about a relief, right?

As I said, the only decision in this system is how much you're going to save before the automatic monthly transfer takes place. And I'm here to help with this, too.

For young adults who want to reach financial freedom sooner and to live life on their terms, I recommend saving 50% of their paycheck or more. That's not a typo—I'm confident you can save 50% of your income (or more depending on how high your salary is). Does that shock you? That's a good place to start.

If you're not used to saving this much, it will probably be overwhelming in the beginning. So one way to help yourself is to slowly increase the percentage each month to build the habit. If you have to start at 25%, then next month save 30%, and so on until you work your way up.

The reason I recommend this high savings percentage is because the more you save, the quicker you will become rich and reach financial freedom. I admit that saving 50% of your paycheck requires some sacrifices, but the freedom to retire at age 35 is completely worth it.

So maybe you can save 50% of your paycheck or maybe you can't, but I like to think big, raise the bar high, and go for it. Sometimes the best way to motivate someone is to shock them out of their current reality.

And imagine if you save 60%, 70%, or more of your income, hello freedom at age 30 maybe?

For those of you who are mad that you have to save this much, you're going to question is it worth it? But, I believe it's entirely worth it to save up front as a twentysomething. Because if you're not willing to sacrifice saving more money now, then you're essentially sacrificing your future freedom and happiness later on. Plus, you're making yourself work for the rest of your life in a job you most likely only do for the money. No one wants to be stuck in that situation. That's why sacrifices right now, and over time, are absolutely worth it.

For example, I strategically decided to move back in with my parents after school for the short-term. I didn't have to, and I can afford a downtown apartment if I really wanted it, but I value financial freedom more. And because I live at home, I'm able to save more than 75% of my income. Then I invest the large majority of this money, so it works for me to make me more money.

At times it's hard and there are thoughts of missing out, but then I shake it off and know I'm doing the right thing for my financial freedom and happiness. Call me a loser or a weirdo for living at home, but you'll never call me poor.

Now Is The Time For High Savings

Now I'm going to show you how many working years you can cut off by increasing your savings percentage. In this example, assume this young adult makes $60,000 a year, which comes to a monthly income of around $3,800 after taxes and medical insurance—a net annual income of $45,600.

Income: $45,600

Year	Savings rate 10%	Savings rate 20%	Savings rate 50%
1	$4,560	$9,120	$22,800
5	$22,800	$45,600	$114,000
10	$45,600	$91,120	$228,000
20	$91,200	$182,400	$456,000

After 20 years of working, the person who saves 20% has two times as much money as the person saving 10% of their money. And the person who went above and beyond to save 50% of their income has five times as much money as the person saving 10% over the 20 years.

More than that, the person saving 50% will be ready to retire around age 42 if they start working at 22. You might say $456,000 isn't enough to retire, and it may or may not be, but we haven't factored in an interest rate and compound interest yet. Assuming this $456,000 is invested with a 7% annual return each year, you're looking at a little over $1,000,000 from only working 20 years. Hello freedom! Plus, we didn't factor in increases in your income, which is likely to happen when you've been working for 20 years.

So, while the 50% saver is retired at age 42 after only 20 years of work, the person saving 20% of their income will have to work 32 total years (when assuming a 7% return rate and compound interest) to reach the same million-dollar total at age 54. That's a difference of 12 years. You know how much happiness the 50% saver experienced in those 12 years of freedom.

And the person saving 10% of their income, to reach around $1,000,000, will have to work 41 years when assuming a 7% return rate and compound interest. Compared to the person who saved 50% of their income, the 10% income saver had to work 21 more years and retire at 63 instead of 42.

When you think saving money isn't worth it, remember that the more you save, the less you have to work. So save as much as you can until money doesn't matter, and you can enjoy unbelievable freedom and satisfaction for the rest of your life. Here's how to accomplish that lifestyle and it starts by paying yourself first.

How To Automatically Pay Yourself First

It's super easy to automatically pay yourself by setting up a monthly electronic transfer from your checking account to your savings account.

For your own good, I really want you to use an online savings account from a bank different than your checking account. For example, I use Capital One 360 for my savings account and a different bank for my checking. This gives you the advantage of making it harder to transfer money from your savings to your checking account. And this makes it more difficult to spend money and helps you save more, which is the goal.

If you're wisely using an online savings account with a bank different than your checking account, you can quickly link your accounts by typing in your bank information.

After the accounts are linked, here's what you do to automatically pay yourself first. You simply select how much money you're going to transfer, on what day the transfer hits (1st of the month, 15th of the month, etc.) and how often the transfer happens (biweekly, monthly, annually). I recommend setting the transfer to take place the day after you get paid and monthly.

Once you do these things, that's it! You've just made an absolutely huge move to get rich and find freedom. I hope you realize the importance that such an easy step has for your future. I'm so pumped for you!

Five Steps To Master Savings

Now that you're committed and automatically set up for freedom unlike the majority of people, these are the five most critical steps to save as much money as you can—and get closer to a freedom-lifestyle as soon as possible.

1. Live below your income.

Would you rather pretend you're rich or actually be rich? The most basic step in saving money is living below your income and saving the difference. Mentally, this might mean pretending you make a lot less, so you're not tempted to say, "Maybe I can afford this." Besides the movie stars, musicians, and athletes, most rich people are financially disciplined and save a large portion of their income as they go. This is a sure-fire way to grow your net worth.

2. Save for a specific short-term goal.

To really get away from the mindset of saving for the sake of saving, save for something you really want—and then write it down. For one, simply having something in mind will help you save more money and stay focused. Secondly, research has proven that writing down your goals significantly increases the chances of you accomplishing them. So pick a specific goal you're saving for, such as: getting out of debt in three years, reaching a net worth of $100,000 in five years, or whatever else could get you motivated. Then write this goal down somewhere you will see it daily.

3. Planners prosper.

Beyond the short-term goals, people who have a long-term plan of what they want their life to be like almost always save more money than those who don't plan. If you truly desire and plan to retire at 40, travel on a boat, sleep in whenever you want, or get to a net worth of $5 million, plan for it. That way, you create an internal why-factor that will motivate you to save more and cut down on unnecessary spending. If you don't have a future plan, short-term gratification is going to win out because it's there and your future is hazy.

4. Build an emergency fund.

Before we get to this step, I want to say that if you have credit card or student loans debt, then do not contribute to an emergency fund. Treat that debt as your emergency and knock it down to zero. In other cases, if you have no debt and want to sleep easier at night, read this tip below:

Emergencies like receiving a hospital bill that insurance doesn't cover, your car breaking down, or losing your job can happen to you. And probably when you don't expect it. These are not as big of a deal if you have money stored away in an online savings account. But, they can injure your financial situation if you're unprepared.

To avoid these nightmares, I would start with a goal of getting to $1,000 for your emergency fund. Set up an automatic monthly transfer from your checking account to an online savings account. Then, if you're really risk averse, save up to 6 months of your living expenses.

5. Saving more lets more money work for you.

Especially as a young adult with a smaller net worth, how much you save is largely going to determine how much money you can invest in the stock market. I enjoy thinking of the process in three steps: the more you save, equals the more you can invest, which turns into more "shares of employees" working to make money for you. Automatically save, automatically invest, and watch your net worth grow as you sit on your butt. It's actually that easy!

Action Steps

Although the later chapter on investing is my favorite and holds the biggest secrets to a freedom-lifestyle, you won't have money to invest if you don't save enough. Plus, you can't control the stock market, but you can control how much you save. Your future is counting on these action steps:

☐ Decide your savings percentage (I recommend 50%, but the higher you can the better).

☐ Set up automatic transfers to an online savings account from your checking account to pay yourself first.

☐ Determine a specific short-term goal and long-term plan to help you save more.

Chapter 5

Spending With A Plan

One of my friends is a good looking guy. He's tall, has a nice smile, and all the girls find him charming. He takes advantage of his natural "talents" and finds himself talking to multiple pretty girls at the same time, all the time. By multiple girls, I mean anywhere from five to ten. It's ridiculous! He basically has a basketball roster of girls, and if he loses interest in one then he adds another one to the team just like that. I'm not saying it's right, I'm saying that's how it is.

He obviously sees attractive qualities in all of them and they all enjoy his attention, not knowing he talks the same way to the other girls. Sounds like the life for you guy readers, right? Or if you're a girl, then reverse the role and think of how cool it would be to have all these options.

Everything goes smooth for a while and he's having fun. But, guess what? Because he's talking to so many different girls, sooner or later things always backfire on him.

For example, two different girls will want to hang out on the same night. Then he either can't pick one so he hangs out with neither of them. Or even when he does pick one, he has to lie to the others and stress over whether they believe him or not. Then he feels guilty the whole night with the girl he's with and has to hide his phone so she doesn't see the texts and Snapchats from the other girls.

He's always being sketchy and trying to cover his tracks to the point that he can't have a good time with one girl and a clear conscience.

What he thought would be a great idea with all these girls is actually constant chaos, where he has to worry and put in the effort to hide the truth with five to ten girls. It wears him out and gives him regular headaches. He thinks his decisions will make him happy, but he's not at the end of the day.

My Friend's Problem Is Also Your Spending Problem

My friend's real problem is he continues to do things with girls that doesn't make him happy. Instead of picking one girl, he thinks wanting them all and living in the moment will make him happier. But then it always ends in him feeling stressed, crappy, and unhappy as he's back to where he started. If he became smart and spent his energy on one girl, then his life would be way more peaceful. Plus, he could happily enjoy the one relationship. I try to give him advice but he's not as good at listening as he is at attracting women. I'm sure you can relate with your friends.

Anyway, I promise my story has relevance to you and your spending habits. The point is that your spending habits are most likely the equivalent of my friend who tries to manage different girls because he wants them all.

Your spending habits show that you want all these different things and you want them now. You want the morning sit down breakfast and latte, the Panera lunch, the fancy dinner, the new shoes (Yeezy sneakers, anyone?), and the expensive clothes. But here's the thing:

those items never give you lasting happiness. Plus, things don't get better when you get your credit card bill at the end of the month and spent way more than you can afford.

Now you're stressed out until your next paycheck comes, because you mismanaged your money and you're not any happier. But, since you don't have a plan or better solution (like my friend), you do the same thing next month. If you keep spending money that way, you'll be in the same unhappy and less rich situation.

Since this unplanned and stressful lifestyle continues to over-promise happiness and underdeliver, let's change it up. Instead of spending money on things that steal from your future freedom and riches, let's do what my player-friend should do. He would be happier picking one girl and focusing on her in his future. You too will better enjoy life and become rich by picking one area to spend money on that actually makes you happier, and then aggressive-ly cutting costs on everything else you can do without. To really break this down, let's look at the difference between how an average person spends money and how a rich person spends money.

The Average Person's Spending Mindset

Right now you probably have an average mindset toward money, like most people. You look to spend money on things that will give you lasting happiness. But, when the after-purchase feeling of joy goes away, as it always does, it leaves you wanting more. The void needs to be filled, over and over.

But at some point, reality is going to set in. You'll realize that noth-ing you bought will provide any long-term happiness. And you'll have less money to your name.

Because when you look to spending money on material things as a means to bring lasting happiness to your life, you sabotage your journey to financial freedom, becoming rich, and a satisfying life.

For those who have a plan for how they spend their money and think long-term, the world opens up for them.

The Rich Person's Spending Mindset

Here's the difference between an average mindset and a rich mindset: rich people have a plan for what they spend their money on and forecast long-term. Essentially, they use their financial intelligence to get ahead of the rat race so they can spend their time doing things they enjoy. The middle-class and poor can't spend their time doing what they enjoy, because they're forced to spend their time making money.

The biggest reason rich people are able to get richer and not struggle is they know the difference between assets and liabilities, and they buy assets.

The difference is simply that an asset makes you richer and a liability takes money out of your account. Assets include things like stocks, businesses, and knowledge, all things that will appreciate your net worth over time. This is where the focus should be. Liabilities will depreciate your net worth over time and include things like cars, mortgages, and credit card debt.

The rich forecast long-term by spending their money on assets that make them money, and gain freedom because of it.

Your Spending Solution

Here's what you need to do. You're probably aware by now that your spending habits need an overhaul. It's time to admit that and actually change. Look at your daily spending and figure out what needs trimming, and identify your bad habits. Admit that spending money on material items doesn't make you happier for the long-term. I've been there, and I know it's true.

There are certain things, besides money, that are scientifically proven to make you happier: freedom, meaningful work, health, family, and a community of friends. So why don't we focus on using our money to get more time with what makes us happier, and live an amazingly satisfying life?

So let this be your spending creed: I'm not going to spend money on things that don't provide lasting happiness, so I can save money to spend time on experiences that do provide lasting happiness.

Anytime you're about to buy something you don't need, ask yourself if this purchase contributes to your freedom and happiness or does it take those two things away.

To really understand what this will do for your life, think of every dollar you spend now in the perspective of future dollars. Rich people, as I'll show below, understand and maximize the greatest power of their assets: compound interest.

Check this out.

If you can spend $10 less a day (same as saving $10 a day), this will give you about $310 a month. Take a look at this chart to see what happens when you invest $310 a month with a 10% annual return:

    1 year = $3,720
    5 years = $22,711
    10 years = $59,287
    20 years = $213,063
    40 years = $1,646,444

Look at that, cut $10 a day off your spending and you have a cool $1.6 million in 40 years. Does eating out all the time and buying a new car instead of a used car sound better than $1.6 million in the future? When you'll then be able to leverage that money to buy you time to enjoy experiences and live better, maybe without caring about making an income so you don't need a job. Or you pursue a job or project that makes you happy regardless of how much it pays.

If you took it a step further and spent $20 less a day, $620 a month (at a 10% return), you would give even more juice to the power of compound interest:

1 year = $7,440
5 years = $45,422
10 years = $118,574
20 years = $426,126
40 years = $3,292,889

Heck with being a millionaire, now you're a multimillionaire with $3.3 million dollars of freedom in your pocket at your disposal. Sounds good, doesn't it?

And for the top-achievers who want to push their spending discipline for maximum rewards, see how far they get by making and saving enough to invest $50 a day, which is $1,550 a month (with 10% return).

1 year = $18,600
5 years = $113,555
10 years = $296,436
20 years = $1,065,315
40 years = $8,232,222

As you can see, the less you spend equals the more you can save and invest, unleashing the power of compound interest and your rich future. You can only imagine the potential if you invested even more money per year. Then we're talking about $10,000,000 plus. Bam!

Whatever your situation is, I realize that many readers wish they had more money to invest each month than they do. If that's the case, then I recommend you go back to Chapter 1 and use one of the strategies to increase your income. If you have the will, you'll find a way! This phrase is a cliche for a reason, because it's true.

Easiest Way To Track Your Spending

Just as saving to save is never going to work, tracking your money only to track it won't work either. But, I believe tracking your money each month isn't so bad, and is completely doable, if planning your spending means the opportunity to make millions of dollars.

The easiest way to track your spending, and what I use, is Mint. com. With Mint.com, you can manage all your spending in a quick, user-friendly, and free manner. Meaning you don't need to collect receipts and punch a calculator each month to total up your spending.

Mint is extremely easy to set-up. All you need to do is connect to your bank accounts and credit cards, and then plan out your monthly spending one time on the Budgets tab. You can add a monthly spending target on categories like gas, food, rent, and entertainment. That way, you can track how you're meeting those targets as you go.

Based on the activity with your linked credit cards and bank accounts, Mint will automatically track your spending for you and show your monthly progress. I find it extremely helpful and motivating to know if I cut cost in an area I don't care as much about, like going out to eat, then I have more money to invest, which will help me reach financial freedom.

Action Steps

These are the action steps to get your spending to align with your present and future happiness.

☐ Have a rich person's spending mindset (buy less liabilities, more assets).

☐ Find areas to cut costs from your spending categories so you have more money to invest for freedom.

☐ Track your spending on Mint.com each week (Sundays work best for me).

Chapter 6

Investing Truths And Myths

Yes! You've made it to the investing chapters and I'm fired up! The saving and spending chapters are simply appetizers, like salad and bread, that prepare you to become rich, but investing your money is the main course. Think about that juicy steak.

In this chapter, you will learn about smart investing choices to maximize returns by minimizing fees. And then in the following two chapters I'll cover how to set your investments on autopilot with occasional check-ins to make yourself rich. I'm not joking. It's as easy as I say it is!

You will see how we're going to get money to work for you and then get out of its way.

First, let's start like we usually do by building your financial intelligence with the reason why you need to invest your money to become rich.

You Don't Have To Be Rich To Invest, But You Have To Invest To Become Rich

The best thing you can do to put yourself in the driver's seat to millions is to invest your money. Even if you already have millions, you're a fool if you don't invest your money in some shape or form.

"But, wait a minute," you say, "Don't you have to have a lot of money to even begin investing?" Little do you know that this is the single biggest lie that trips up young adults from investing and costs them big sums of money. This lie causes people to delay investing, work longer, live a more stressful life, and lose out on the freedom to live on their own terms.

Before I show you why investing right away is so critical, I want to say one more thing: I've gone to the future and talked to your future self. (You look good, besides your haircut that could use some work, unless that's the style of the future.)

Your future self gave me a direct message to forward to you, "Start investing now, even if it's small. If you wait to invest later in life, you're going to regret it and be significantly more poor."

Then as I left, the future you told me that you're stubborn and will also need to see the below chart on compound interest (which means interest paid on both the initial investment sum and on the interest it has earned) before you would come around. Here it is:

Age	Yearly Contribution	Investment Return	Total value At 65
22	$5,000	8%	$1,647,915
23	$5,000	8%	$1,521,218
24	$5,000	8%	$1,403,905
25	$5,000	8%	$1,295,283
26	$5,000	8%	$1,194,706
27	$5,000	8%	$1,101,578
28	$5,000	8%	$1,015,350

Age	Yearly Contribution	Investment Return	Total value At 65
29	$5,000	8%	$935,509
30	$5,000	8%	$861,583

As you see, waiting five years to invest at age 27 instead of age 22 costs you $546,337 at age 65. That's a big chunk of change! Waiting seven years to start investing at 29 costs you nearly a million dollars.

You know, if you talk to any older adults about investing (like I have), the first thing they almost always say is that they wish they started investing sooner and they wish they ignored the lie that you need lots of money to start investing. Well, guess what? You could repeat those mistakes, or you can learn from the mistakes of others to get a treasure chest of money.

Your future self, some old-timers, and myself aren't the only ones who say you should start investing as much money as you can now, and then let compound interest take over to make you a boatload of money over time.

There's also someone named Albert Einstein, not considered the dumbest guy on the block, who said, "Compound interest is the eighth wonder of the world. He who understands it, earns it...he who doesn't...pays it." And Einstein even went further to say, "The most powerful force in the universe is compound interest." Those are big claims from a bright man.

If you're not convinced by this chart and this genius's vote of confidence, then nothing else I say or show you will persuade you because Einstein completely nailed it. Thanks for the help Albert. I wish I could get a beer with that guy.

When we turn the biggest lie of investing upside down (that you should wait until you have more money and you're around 35), for its truth (that investing right away is huge, even if it's small in the beginning), then we gain the greatest investment advantage: decades of compound interest.

You saw in the chart above how a couple dollars a day with compound interest can turn into hundreds of thousands of dollars in the future. So we've established that a few dollars a day can have significant importance to your money. With the same reasoning, cutting unnecessary costs to save dollars now is also huge.

That's why this next section is all about avoiding the bad investments to help you cut unnecessary costs and increase your investing performance. Everything about investing is only going to become more clear the further we go. You got this!

Unnecessary Weight Part 1: Mutual Funds

A mutual fund is a fund made up of different individual stocks. The banks and your financial adviser all love mutual funds. The reason? They make a killing off of mutual funds. So they sell the (true) advantages of investing in a mutual fund like: relieving the responsibility of picking your own individual stocks; getting solid diversification compared to a few individual stocks; and having a professional actively managing your money. Because when you buy a mutual fund, you give the fund's manager your money to make the best investment decisions based off of his research and knowledge.

There is positive marketing everywhere about mutual funds, which is why the common investor also loves putting their money in mutual funds.

But, this hands off approach where an "expert" manages your money comes at a cost, and is the reason mutual funds aren't all they're cracked up to be. The media, big banks, and your financial adviser talk less about this part. Mutual funds are most often expensive as they charge around 2% in annual fees. These fees can cover anything from the fund manager's salary, brokerage fees, research costs, and administrative expenses. And they unfairly make you pay the price for these fees every year, regardless of performance. If the fund is down 5% in performance for a year, you're down 7% because of mutual fund fees.

And that's not even the worst part.

The alarming problem is most actively managed mutual funds don't beat passively managed index funds in performance for the long term. For reference, mutual funds are designed to beat the S&P 500, which is made up of 500 large public companies in the U.S whose performance is considered representative of the entire stock market. On the other hand, index funds are designed to match the S&P 500. Some of the reason for mutual fund's underperformance is due to the fees that we already covered, but also because it's extremely difficult for mutual fund managers to consistently pick stocks that outperform the whole market. To sum it up, mutual funds are expensive and underperform the market average.

The other option I mentioned, index funds, is what I'll cover in-depth in the next chapter. But, right now realize you can get an expense ratio of around 0.17% with index funds, compared to 2% with mutual funds.

Since small percentage points can make it difficult to grasp the big picture, take a look at the following chart to see the difference in expenses between mutual funds and index funds:

Investment total	Annual mutual fund 2% expenses	Annual index fund 0.17% expenses
$10,000	$200	$17
$50,000	$1,000	$85
$100,000	$2,000	$170
$250,000	$5,000	$425
$1,000,000	$20,000	$1,700

With $10,000 in your stock portfolio, the index fund costs you $183 less a year. With $100,000 in investments, an index fund is $1,830 cheaper than a mutual fund. And with investments of $1,000,000, the index fund is $18,300 cheaper. Since these are expenses that occur every year, this is essentially compound interest working against you over time when you choose a mutual fund instead of an index fund.

Don't forget: these mutual funds are not only more expensive, but they also usually underperform the market index funds.

Unnecessary Weight Part 2: Financial Advisers

Financial advisers are in the same basket as mutual funds. What you think you get in the security and letting an "expert" help you with your decisions will often cost you more than help you.

Firstly, you usually have to pay financial advisers anywhere around 2% to manage your money and give you advice. Secondly, these advisers might not always have your best interest in mind. Many times they are paid off of commission fees, so they will advise you to put your money in expensive investment funds, like mutual funds, to get paid extra commission in addition to the 2% flat fee.

And most shocking, financial advisers are no better than fund managers at beating the market and picking winning investments. For example, NerdWallet.com did a study that found only 24% of professional investors have beaten the market over the past 10 years. So you're paying more money to financial advisers, and most often getting a worse return than if you took the market. This underperformance can cost you anywhere from tens of thousands to hundreds of thousands of dollars or maybe even millions over a lifetime, which is not cool.

Are there any advantages to having a financial adviser for your investments? My only answer is that they can be helpful if you're insanely busy and you don't have time for investing money. Or if you have double-digit sources of income streams you can't manage. Or if you need assistance planning when to take money out of your trust fund. Since these three scenarios are all extremely rare, the super-majority of young adults can do better on their own without the expensive and underperforming financial adviser. A financial adviser might be needed later down the road, but not right now.

Being on your own might be scary for some of you, but your investing needs won't be so complex that you're lost in details and decisions. If you're able to spend a couple of hours here and there to learn about investing and managing your money, that's all you need to set yourself up to succeed. Plus, you'll feel more secure and have more confidence when you know your way around your investments. Rather than trusting your future with some professional investor who may have ulterior motives for where to send your money, take the full responsibility and reins for your wealth and financial freedom.

Don't worry if you feel unequipped, you won't be left in the ocean with only this advice. I'm going to bring you to shore with all the basics you need to know for your financial security and wealth.

Chapter 7

Your Winning Investment Strategy

We've covered what you don't want with your investments, now it's time to cover what you want.

For clarity, I decided to break this chapter into three parts: Part I: Why An Index Fund Is Your Best Bet, Part II: What About Buying Individual Stocks?, and Part III: Putting It All Together.

Part I: Why An Index Fund Is Your Best Bet

I remember being the best basketball player in my middle school, and I'm not trying to brag because it's middle school. Also, that's not saying much as no one from that school went past high school basketball to play college or professional ball. But anyway, the point is I was the best player, and cocky about it.

So when recess came for the daily basketball game, I decided to pick some of my friends to play against the other players, knowing my friends weren't as good. I still thought my team would win because of me.

And then we lost the first day, the next day, and all week. It sucked week after week, and I didn't even have fun playing anymore because we kept losing. Instead of quitting, I decided to do something different. I joined the other team. And because of that one move, I instantly got the joy of playing basketball back as I started to win all the time.

How does this apply to your investing strategy? When I switched from the losing basketball team to the winning team, I had to accept that my first plan of relying only on my talent didn't work. It's a classic example of if you can't beat them, then you might as well join them. And by "them," I mean the winning team. Same goes for where you put your money. An index fund, what I invest in and recommend to all young adult investors, uses the same strategy: if you can't beat the market, then you might as well join the market.

For your 401k, IRA or Roth IRA, and beginning investments when starting from scratch, an index fund is your best bet to set up a foundation of investing success. In other words, it's your best bet toward optimizing freedom. Partly mentioned above, index funds literally match the market, with the market usually meaning the S&P 500 or Dow Jones Industrial Average. If you read an online headline with "the market" in the title, or you hear people on tv talking about "the stock market," it's almost definitely referring to the S&P 500 or the Dow Jones. And the S&P 500 is made up of 500 large companies in the United States, so Facebook, Apple, Amazon, etc. And the Dow Jones is made up of 30 significant publicly owned United States companies, like Disney, Microsoft, Wal-Mart, etc.

The first reason an index fund is great for you is because of their low expense ratios. You already heard me go on about how expensive mutual funds are, with a cost of around 2% in fees, because they're actively managed. And mutual funds also commonly include commission or sales charges on top of them, which take more money from you and some of that gets paid to the financial planners. Again, it's unfair, lame, and not cool.

However, since index funds are passively managed, you can get solid index funds for less than 0.2% in costs and they don't include sales or commission fees. So, index funds let you keep more of the profit, and don't send extra money to financial planners or mutual fund managers.

Secondly, and where index funds shine, is in most cases over the past decades index funds (who mimic the S&P 500 index) straight up beat mutual funds in performance.

I'm not saying that every single index fund beats every single mutual fund, because that would be an overgeneralization. Especially over the short term, there are going to be mutual funds that do better than the market. The only problem? It's nearly impossible to pick the small group of winning mutual funds out of the thousands to choose from.

So my main point is this: because it's extremely difficult to pick specific stocks to outperform the market and because of all the extra costs with mutual funds, index funds outperform the vast majority of mutual funds. When choosing a path to freedom, index funds provide the fastest route.

And it's not that mutual funds are a terrible investment, because they're actually a better investment over time than sitting on the sidelines with your money. But their heavy costs hamper their performance and make them look ugly compared to index funds.

If you're not convinced already, I'm not finished supporting index funds. Since a classic move of smart authors is using other smart people to back them up, I might as well join them. So here is what some of the best investors have to say about index funds:

> *"By periodically investing in an index fund, the know-nothing investor can actually out-perform most investment professionals." - Warren Buffett, billionaire who is regarded as the best investor of all time*

With the needle meaning specific stocks or mutual funds, and the haystack meaning an index fund:

> *"Don't look for the needle. Buy the haystack." - John Bogle, founding father of index funds and founder of The Vanguard Group*

And to put it bluntly about why you should choose an index fund over a mutual fund:

> *"If you're investing in mutual funds you're most likely, well, to put it delicately—how about 'getting hosed.'" - Jim Cramer, host of CNBC's Mad Money and former hedge fund manager*

I had a tough time narrowing it down to only three quotes from successful investors who love index funds because there was many to choose from. But, since you get the point, I'll wrap it up.

Index funds have extremely low expenses and beat the vast majority of mutual funds over time. That's why index funds are the perfect starting place for your first investments and the majority of your investment money.

Are index funds too good to be true? Well there is one critique against passively managed index funds, which says that they are more volatile than an actively managed mutual fund. You'll see why the point is highly irrelevant though, if not entirely irrelevant, with your investing strategy as a young adult.

Are Index Funds Too Good To Be True?

Before we bring it all together and summarize your winning investment strategy, let's first address the one concern about index funds, which is their short-term volatility. Assuming you're in your twenties, the reason this short-term volatility concern isn't really a risk is because you have decades before you will need your money.

If you're 60, then your number one focus will be on protecting your wealth and you'll focus less on growing it. At this age, you can't afford a huge market recession if you're only invested in stocks because you might not have the energy to work or you might have expensive medical bills on the horizon. But, last time I checked, this book is for young adults and not senior citizens.

For young adults like you and I, we shouldn't care as much about the short-term risk because we are focused on building wealth over the long haul. If the market goes down 20%, and we keep our money in it (which is the only solution since time in the market is our only advantage), then we will get the recovery when it most likely goes back up. If we take our money out after a 20% loss, then we'll almost definitely miss the recovery and that's miserable. So the lesson is to keep your money in the market, almost always.

We will get the most out of our money (to a certain degree) by going with the motto: higher potential risk equals higher potential reward. As a twentysomething, if you have your money in bonds or completely out of the market, you're just wasting opportunity for returns as you're way too conservative.

For my extra conservative and skeptical readers, let this fact about investing ease your worries: Dating back from 1926 to 2015, so over the last 89 years, the S&P 500 (the market) has produced negative returns in only 24 years compared to the positive returns in 65 of the years. What's more meaningful is in this timespan, the overall return is around 10%, which is the beauty of index funds.

And since 1926, there's never been a single 20-year stretch where an investor has lost money with a diversified investment of large US firms (essentially an index fund). So if you can stay in the market with your index fund, through the ups and downs, history says you're going to make good money.

That's why I believe the core of your investment portfolio needs to match the market with an index fund! There's no question about it.

Part II: What About Buying Individual Stocks?

Changing gears here, there's another investment possibility that we haven't explicitly discussed. Buying individual stocks is something else you can do with your investment portfolio to create wealth.

Individual stocks are a different animal, as they have the potential to soar and plummet in a short time period. For example, their value can go up and down by double-digit percent in a matter of days. Also, as mutual funds find it harder to beat index funds because they have to pick the right stocks out of thousands to choose from, the same rules apply to you when picking individual stocks. It's extremely hard to pick winning stocks more times than not, so be careful.

But if you're first well-rooted with $10,000 in a market index fund and this index continues to make up 90% of your overall investment money, then you can potentially add another strategy. This is what I do, although I've been wrong thousands of times in my life, so don't feel like you have to do this or I'm pushing this. But, with the other 10% of my total investment money outside of the index funds, I buy individual stocks with the goal that these shares turn into a home run.

What's an investing home run? It's when you buy shares of a company, and then the shares take off like a banshee giving you big returns on your initial investment.

Sometimes you catch a shooting star and the shares go up 1,000% or more. For example, companies like Tesla, Netflix, Apple, and Google are all up over 1,000% after going public. That's insane! So if you follow my strategy, your goal with your highflier money is to find the next Tesla or Netflix and buy it before it soars.

Obviously this is easier said than done, but that's part of the fun in it (as long as you have no debt and save a significant portion of your income, you can afford to take chances to dramatically increase your wealth).

Here are some general tips for finding the next stock that breaks the roof, but take my advice with a grain of salt because this is more luck than skill. Many companies look like bad investments before they shock the world and kaboom upward.

To find a highflier stock, I look at companies that:

- Are extremely disruptive to industries or they create an industry of their own (think of companies with a potential to become a monopoly)

- Have the potential to get their product or service in the hands of every consumer on the planet

- Leverage new technology to change the status quo

Then the idea is you swoop in and buy shares when they're in the double digits (but sometimes even at triple digits) without much attention, and then you hold on until the company finds unbelievable growth as the shares gain 30%, 50%, 100%, and beyond.

Since you're holding onto these individual stocks for 25-plus years, buying stocks isn't as risky and is certainly not a get rich quick mindset I rallied against in Chapter 2. However, day trading stocks would be an unwise get rich scheme for 99.99% of people. Because you're competing against computers who trade on milliseconds and you need to be an expert of experts to make money in this arena.

Plus, remember that since your first $10,000 and 90% of your total investment money is compounding in index funds, you can give yourself the freedom to go big with your extra money and you won't be financially left for dead if you swing and miss (assuming you completed the earlier strategies laid out in this book).

If picking individual stocks and the idea of watching the value go down by 30% makes you nauseous, you have no interest in business, or you literally can't make time to do research, then it may be better off to put 100% of your investment money in index funds. There's no weakness in that, it may even make everyone who bought potential flier stocks look dumb if their share price never soars.

Part III: Putting It All Together

To summarize, here's a winning investment strategy in my opinion:

1. Put your first $10,000 and then 90% of your total invested money (at all times) in an S&P 500 index fund.

For your individual retirement accounts like your 401k, IRA (no tax when you contribute, taxed when you withdraw the money) or Roth IRA (taxed when you contribute the money, no tax at withdrawal), I recommend buying an index fund that mimics the S&P

500. This way you get shares of the best 500 companies in the United States, which is a safe investment for your future and this protects against inflation.

I'm currently invested in VFIAX, which is the Vanguard 500 Index Admiral Class and mimics the S&P 500 market. I like this Vanguard fund because of its low 0.05% cost while similar funds in the same category are over 1.00% in fees and expenses.

And there are two reasons I recommend you put the first $10,000 you invest in an index fund. For one, it's common for index funds to require a minimum balance of $10,000 to get the lowest expense ratio and lowest fees. (The VFIAX I mentioned requires a minimum of $10,000.)

Secondly, I find that $10,000 is a good short-term goal to shoot for and hit the ground running with buying your first investment. It's certainly reachable with a full-time income and when you have financial discipline in your savings and spending.

To buy this index fund, see if where you work offers an employee match program where the company essentially gives you free money toward your investment. And buy an S&P 500 index fund in this account, if one is available, with low expenses and fees.

If your work doesn't have a match program or offer an index fund as an option, you can get one on your own through companies like Fidelity, Vanguard, Schwab, and T. Rowe Price. Set up an account if you haven't, then there should be a 'Trade' button to click on, and type in the symbol of your index fund and the $10,000 you're investing to get set up. Then hit 'Buy' and hold that money in there for decades.

As you get in your 40s and 50s and 60s, you will want a less aggressive and therefore different investment plan that also prioritizes protecting your wealth. Dividend stocks, CD accounts, and other options are helpful in this area. But this book is for young adults, so I won't go too in-depth with that.

2. Buy individual stocks that have the potential to rocket to the moon, but allocate no more than 10% of your total investment money here.

After you've taken care of business with your index fund, it's time for the fun part. This is where you can buy individual stocks, if you want. I recommend taking fliers on companies with big ideas, often these are new technology companies with the potential to explode skyward.

Once you've picked your favorite flier stock, (assuming you set up an individual investment account outside of your work) log in to the same investment account that holds your index fund. Then click on a tab that will read something like 'Trade' or 'Trade Stocks.' Simply type in the company's name, or stock ticker symbol (validate you have the right one first), with how many shares you want to buy and click 'Purchase.' Then all you can do is patiently wait and hope you picked a winner. Or continue to buy shares, and then wait to see how the shares perform.

With all this said, if you're extra conservative and you get sick to your stomach at the thought of losing money, it's perfectly fine to ignore this step and put all of your investment money in an index fund. I'm personally more of a risk taker, especially at age 23, so going 100% in an index fund isn't my strategy. Either way, when you buy stock, it's almost always in your best interest to hold onto it for decades.

Action Steps

Take these action steps to put your investment portfolio together:

☐ Determine your investing style and strategy: either 100% of your investment money in an index fund, or 90% index and 10% individual stocks.

☐ Buy $10,000 worth of shares in an S&P 500 index fund to get the power of compound interest working for you.

☐ If you're up for it, research and buy individual stocks that could potentially soar (but put no more than 10% of your total investments in these stocks).

Chapter 8

Feed The Investing Machine

People that know me always ask things like, "How do you find the time to write two books in six months?," "How are you so productive at blogging?" and, "What's your secret to being consistent all the time?"

Besides the main motivating factors like I love sharing what I've learned with people, improving my habits to better myself, and trying to get the most out of every day, there's something else that would surprise people.

You know what it is? I'm actually a big believer in the idea of working hard now, so I can be lazy later. I dig in for long days in the present, with the belief that my work will pay off in the future without needing any more effort from me.

I know myself and it seems like I would rather go insane than fall into a spell of laziness. But the possibility of losing my energy as I age and having nothing to keep producing results for me is scary.

I work hard up front to set up systems so I can give my attention to other areas, say freedom.

Automatic Investing

You have the right investing strategy and gameplan, now it's time to execute. Once you pick your index fund, although it's almost entirely hands off, you still need to contribute money every month. And that can be difficult as life is sometimes busy and messy. For example, you can forget to send money to your fund, or you can spend too much so you don't have enough to contribute that month.

But, remember the power of compound interest? Without consistently sending money to your index fund, compound interest can only go so far when it has little to work with.

However, if you continue to feed money to the machine of compound interest, it will start working harder and harder for you to make you rich sooner. Through compound interest, every dollar you invest now will make you more in the future.

So how do we stay consistent to make our monthly investments? It's called automatic investing, and you're going to love it.

When you automate your investments, you immediately take away any discipline problems, bad decisions based off of emotion, and make it incredibly easy for you to invest without any trouble.

This is because automatic investing is exactly what it says it is, automatic. Besides the initial set up, it's entirely hands off to the point where you don't even have to think about it. When the day comes every month that you assigned, say the 15th of every month, money will be taken from your checking account to your investment fund.

This will psychologically help you feed the investment machine that's going to make you rich. You will never forget to contribute. And gone are the times when you can say, "Oh, I'll do it next month," or, "I spent too much, so I can't invest this month." This system holds you accountable to spend less so you have enough to contribute because you know the money is being automatically taken out.

And automatic investing keeps going regardless of whether the market is up or down, which is what you want or your emotions will get in the way. You keep on contributing every month no matter if the stock market is high or low.

So even if you have to start automatically investing with only $100 a month, I recommend getting started and slowly increasing your contributions over time. When you do small increases, I bet you'll barely notice a difference from month to month in your checking account. However, your investment fund is using every dollar to work harder for you. Soon, your $100 a month can turn into investing $300, $500, $1,000 a month, and more if you continue increasing your contributions as your income increases over time.

To get started, log in to your investment account. Then search for a link or tab that mentions something like automatic investing, automatic transfers, scheduled investments, or a similar phrase. It should be within sight on the homepage. (If you can't find it, give customer service a call.) Assuming your bank account is already linked, type the amount you're going to contribute each month and the date it's going to be transferred from your bank to the index fund. Now, you're set up, and one step closer to freedom.

With automatic investing, your account grows, compound interest produces more return, and your net worth is unleashed to new heights! That's why if you can save more money by cutting unnecessary expenses on what won't make you happier in the long run, you can invest more.

And by investing more in your twenties, you shorten the time it takes you to become rich. Meaning you fast-track the road to choosing what you spend your time on, enjoying experiences, and getting freedom to live the life you desire.

However, you won't be able to do automatic contributions when purchasing individual stocks. With those, you'll need to log on to your account and buy them yourself each time. But without counting research, the process of buying the stock you want takes no more than three minutes.

Avoid These Investing Mistakes

You have all you need to get your money working for you through investing. I told you it's not so complicated and you can do better off on your own.

However, because of human nature and how emotional people are with their money, people are prone to making rash decisions that kill their investments. If you want to get the best performance out of your stocks as a young adult, don't commit these mistakes:

Mistake 1: Sell your retirement funds early.

If you don't have a savings account or an emergency fund, for whatever reason, you might be tempted to withdraw money from your retirement fund to pay for something. But, I highly advise you find money from somewhere else and protect your retirement funds like a newborn baby. Because, besides taking on credit card debt, taking money out of your retirement account is one of the worst moves you can make for your financial future. Here's why.

If your withdrawal from your Roth IRA is more than your contributions, the government doesn't like that. So they will hit you with a 10% early withdrawal penalty fee. They also give you the blessing of higher taxes if you sell early because they treat it as income tax. Isn't the government so sweet?

And if the high fees and taxes aren't bad enough, probably the worst part is you're limiting compound interest. Here you have this incredible asset that's working to make you money and it's getting depleted. All of these add up to missed opportunities where you pay for it, literally.

Mistake 2: Sell your index funds when the entire market is down.

Maybe the hardest part in investing is the guts it takes to hold onto your index fund when the market is going down by 10%, 20%, or 30%, and you're helplessly watching your accounts get gashed. Many people don't want to lose more money, so they decide it's best to sell their index fund now and wait for a calmer market.

But, then the market rebounds by 10%, 20%, or 30%, and these same people missed all the gains because their money was out. Let me tell you that not even the Wall Street professionals and hedge fund managers know exactly when the market is going to go back up. So how are you going to know the perfect time to take your money out and put your money in? You're not, so stay patient in the market. Time is on your side.

Considered the best investor of all time, billionaire Warren Buffett said, "Be fearful when others are greedy and be greedy when others are fearful." So next time a financial crisis happens, similar to the 2008 recession, continue buying as usual—or contribute extra money if you can. Then you'll get investments at a cheap value and reap your profits later.

Mistake 3: Check your index funds or the news every day.

Seeing how your investments are doing every day is unwise because it will lead to committing Mistake 1 and Mistake 2. When you check your investments daily, you develop a dangerous short-term mindset. A short-term mindset fails so many investors because it causes them to sell at the wrong time—too early.

Remember one of the key advantages of an index fund is it's low-maintenance. So instead of checking every day, check your index funds once a month. Your investments and compound interest are going to work just as hard for you if you're watching or not watching. Why not get the returns and spend your time doing better things that you enjoy?

And what also doesn't help is to check the stock market headlines each day. The news is the king of short-term thinking, and its fanciful headlines could shock you into selling too early.

Action Steps

These are some of the most important steps in your journey to financial freedom, so pay close attention:

☐ Automate your monthly investment contributions by linking to your checking account so you can focus on better things.

☐ Increase your monthly contributions over time.

☐ Buy and hold regardless of the market's current performance, in other words don't sell your investments early or when the market is down.

Chapter 9

Remember The Goal: Financial Freedom

Congratulations, you're almost finished! Many young adults don't read a single book a year, let alone one about money. So, your initiative to buy, read, and implement the strategies in this book is a major accomplishment that will empower you to master your money over 95% of the world.

In the past eight chapters, we've covered how to become rich and reach freedom through a freedom mindset and wise money management. With your new wisdom, you now have the tools to reach millionaire status and beyond. Your potential is unlimited. A lot of young people think money planning comes later in life. As you've learned, money planning begins as soon as you have money coming in.

But, in your journey to becoming rich, it's crucial that you don't lose sight of the real goal: reaching freedom.

For me, being free allows me to make money doing what I want to do. I don't want to be limited by money. I want to travel where and when I want, give my money to causes bigger than myself, and change the world. Your picture of freedom might be different, and it should be because you're a different person with different interests.

Don't procrastinate or wait another day to start living your life for freedom. When you put off working towards freedom for later, you increase the chances of the Big Lie tricking you, like it tricks millions of people.

This is the Big Lie: You sacrifice your happiness in your 20s, 30s, 40s, and 50s, hoping your future 60s, 70s, and 80s will be worth it in nice vacations and beaches. But, you never experience the true freedom and joy of life because you're financially limited. Why not enjoy life sooner and along the way?

The Big Lie leaves people unhappy on their journey to wealth, and then never gives them the opportunity to get the fruit from their decades of sacrifice. Talk about a wasted effort and a tragic shame.

The way to avoid the Big Lie and find freedom isn't all about working every day to grow your bank account, but actually getting your money to work for you so you can prioritize other stuff above money.

Things Better Than Money

If you really think about it, I'm sure you would agree that many things in life are more important than money. For example, you couldn't put a price tag on some of life's treasures if you tried, like your health, family, friends, memories, laughter, dreams, and happiness.

In fact, all of these things are priceless. And did you notice how nothing I mentioned is a material item? As we went over this idea in the spending chapter, material items only provide short-term happiness and then leave you empty.

And actually, when you give other things more priority in your life than money, the weird thing is you free yourself to earn, save, and invest better to acquire more money. We'll get to this point soon.

If you're honest with yourself, I bet you don't necessarily care for the money or what you can buy with it as much as you desire the feeling of being rich, feeling secure and stable in your financial situation. You want what the money gives you more than the money itself.

And that is perfectly normal. But a lot of people think they have to be rich before they can feel rich. A lot of people think they have to wait a long time before they can afford to prioritize things ahead of money. This isn't true.

Listen to this. What if I told you that you don't have to be rich to get the feeling of being rich? I guarantee you will say, "Yes, I'm in!" Well, I'm not lying, here's how.

Giving Back

Plain and simple, the single best way to feel rich during your journey to wealth is to give back. And what's great is when you do this you get these feelings of inspiration, satisfaction, and joy—that's what you truly want more than money, right?

You aren't limited to only giving money to achieve this rich feeling, because you can also give your time to help others. Volunteer to serve a local organization that could use it.

Before you protest that you don't have enough money or enough time to give back, I challenge you to start small. Start by giving $50 to your favorite charity organization, or spend one hour of your time on a Saturday helping a local group. Then let the results and your feelings snowball to greater generosity.

If you're wondering what I do, I give to one guy who changes lives on college campuses, another who is sharing hope across the world, and then a local organization who provides shelter, food, and rehabilitation to my community. Why do I give? Because it adds to my feeling that my money actually has purpose.

I've set up financial goals, and along these goals are my giving goals. My giving goals include funding a Pencils of Promise school, funding a hospital, or creating my own foundation to address the needs of a particular group—I set the bar high in life because it pushes me to deliver. I have my eyes set on total freedom, and I believe I'll get there.

When you start giving back, you will quickly realize the beauty of giving. The more you give, the better you feel. It will be a fun, healthy addiction and there aren't many healthy addictions. And you know your generosity is the reason that something amazing happened for someone else.

If you're stubborn and still not convinced, understand this: Giving back your money or time can also help your finances.

When you're grateful, you're less likely to suffer from materialism and spend money on impulse purchases, which helps your savings.

And when you see the difference your money makes, you will feel great and want to give more. This desire to give more can translate to a desire to make more money, and thus increase your income. The benefits of giving go full-circle to the receiver and the giver.

With all these reasons, I encourage you to try out giving back. If you hate it, then I'll truly be surprised and you don't have to do it again. But, I'm confident you will feel like a million bucks when you give back and realize your great potential to improve the world.

How To Give Back

If you decide to financially give back, this section is for you.

Remember how you automated your investing, so you can get the results without worrying about any future actions? You can do the same exact autopilot setup for your financial giving.

I set up an automatic monthly contribution that goes through the 24th of every month, like clockwork. It's automated, simple, and I get to smile every time I see the money taken out of my account to help other people.

When you're ready, pick a cause or an organization where you trust their mission and the use of your money. Then set up a monthly contribution that gets taken out of your checking account on a certain day of each month. The simpler the process, the more likely you'll follow through to receive the benefits of giving.

The goal of this book is that you intelligently manage your money, so you not only transform your life and gain freedom, but you also improve the lives of those around you. When you do this, you live a life bigger than yourself, and what's more liberating than that?

Action Steps

These are the action steps to keep you focused on your long-term satisfaction, outside of money:

☐ Determine what freedom and satisfaction means for you and what you value more than money.

☐ Find an organization you believe in and you trust with your money or time.

☐ Schedule a monthly gift or find a regular time to help others and change the world.

Chapter 10

Follow Through For Success

You now have all the information in this book you need to reach financial freedom and live the life of your dreams. But as important as reading this book is to gain financial intelligence to become rich, if you don't spend the time doing the action steps, then this knowledge is basically useless.

I personally have implemented all these money habits into my lifestyle. And rather than being scared about money, I feel empowered because I've taken control of it and I am getting the most out of my income. Since the first time I set up my automatic systems, it's a huge relief to watch them do the trick every month as I become wealthier.

So be a winner and follow through on the action steps in this book to get the same feeling as me. Spend significantly less than you earn, save and invest in index funds as much as you can, and soon enough you will reach financial freedom. The more you save, the quicker you reach freedom day.

Then, you will exit the rat race, and retire decades before other people. You won't have to work for an income anymore, so you're free to stop chasing money. You can focus on pursuing happiness and meaningful work for the rest of your life. That's the kind of life I want. And I know it's possible, because I don't see money as something to think about later. And now, neither do you!

It's great that you're taking care of your own wealth and freedom in your life. However, I'm confident you would feel even better if you passed along what you learned from this book with your friends and family. It makes a huge difference when you have loved ones around you to take on this journey to financial freedom together. That's when it's more rewarding—when your impact becomes bigger than yourself by sharing life-changing information!

Lastly, if this book has helped you and you have a success story (no matter how big or small), I'd love it if you would leave a short review on Amazon. Thank you so much in advance!

More From Brian Robben

Amazon Bestseller - The Golden Resume

Are you struggling to write a successful resume? Are you frustrated with applying to organizations and not getting interviews? Or maybe you are getting interviews, but you struggle to interview well and ultimately get rejected.

No matter your situation, The Golden Resume will show you how to get the big internship or job you desire and deserve, through mastering your resume and acing interviews.

Get The Golden Resume on Amazon right now:
TakeYourSuccess.com/GoldenResume

Learn more about Brian at TakeYourSuccess.com.

www.ingramcontent.com/pod-product-compliance
Lightning Source LLC
Chambersburg PA
CBHW070328190526
45169CB00005B/1794